CONTENTS

Pages 2 and 3: Photo courtesy of Dr. D. Terver, Nancy Aquarium. Page 34 and 35 photo by B. Kahl.

T.F.H. Publications, The Spinney, Parklands, Denmead, Portsmouth PO7 6AR England

Introduction

When we talk about successful plant culture, we mean keeping plants thriving, growing and reproducing. To do this, plants need light, food, water, room to grow, and a little attention.

Plants provide a naturalistic and healthful environment. Through their absorption of minerals and carbon dioxide, plants tend to purify the water. Plants also provide locations in which many fishes feel secure and thus show their best coloration and behavior. Additionally, many plants serve as a source of food for the animals housed with them, and many varieties of fishes rely on plants either for spawning and/or for helping their young survive.

ROOTED PLANTS

The rooted plants are by no means the only aquatic plants with roots, but they are the only plants that *must* grow fixed in the substrate. The five common genera are *Sagittaria* and *Vallisneria*, the tape grasses; *Echinodorus*, the various swordplants; *Aponogeton*, including the lace plant and ruffled sword; and *Cryptocoryne*, the most varied genus of the five.

The basic parts of all these plants are roots, stem, crown and leaves, with each leaf borne up on a petiole, or leaf stem, of varying length. Reproductive structures, whether runners or flower spikes, arise from the crown, as do the leaves, which brings us to the first point of care: when these plants are inserted in the sand, the crown must not be injured or covered. If this happens, growth will be affected adversely, and the plant may even die.

With small- to medium-sized rooted plants, then, it is wise to select exactly where you want the plant to be in the sand and then gently place it on the surface one or two inches away. Then, with a gentle sweeping motion and slight downward pressure, move it to the desired spot. If the end of your index finger is at the crown, it will be properly located above the sand. The roots will be buried for the most part, and those that are not can be gently inserted into the sand.

The second point is to give these plants sufficient room in which to grow. When setting swordplants, *Aponogeton*, and *Cryptocoryne*, allow at least one-third of the height of the adult plant between each plant that is set. With the tape grasses, one- half inch or so is enough. If the single-rooted plants are crowded, their growth and health will suffer, as will that of the neighboring plants with which they share the tank.

There are certain conditions to guard against in the aquarium if one hopes to raise plants successfully.

Foul water will kill fishes rapidly, and it will kill the plants as well, if not as quickly. A foul bottom will be followed by destruction of plant roots. Some fishes are voracious plant eaters. There are also those fishes that will pick plants apart or grub them up repeatedly.

BUNCH PLANTS

Bunch plants have long stems, and their leaves are borne up on them. There is a node at each location from which the leaves emerge; this node is similar to the crown of the single-rooted plants. Either leaves, new shoots, roots or flowers can emerge from the nodes. Thus, the node is to the bunch plant what the crown is to the single-rooted one.

Most varieties of bunch plants do not send out lateral runners over the bottom, but some do. Most bunch plants tend to grow straight up to the surface and then through it into the air. The leaves produced in the air are smaller, denser and sturdier, and are covered with a shiny or waxy cuticle that preserves moisture.

Blooms will occur only on the emersed part of these plants. Seeds can be cultured, but a more effective manner of reproduction is the replanting of cuttings. This can be done when the plant has grown a bit in the aquarium: simply cut or pinch through the stem, taking a piece with one or two nodes that can be put below the surface of the sand and at least four nodes with leaves attached that can be set above the sand surface. Remove leaves from the buried part of the stem. Growth should begin almost at once in the cutting, and sprouts will form from the nodes left on the donor plant, creating a bushier effect, just as pruning does to terrestrial plants.

Bunch plants can be set quite closely together, say one inch or so apart. Indeed they look better set closely and grow quite well under conditions of crowding that would be a setback to the single-rooted varieties. Under this category are to be found the genera *Elodea*, *Limnophila*, *Hygrophila*, *Cabomba*, *Synnema*, and *Ludwigia*.

FLOATING PLANTS

These plants may float on the surface with their roots hanging down in the water, under the surface with the roots free in the water, or—like the various dwarf lilies—rooted in the sand with the leaves floating on the surface or emersed in the water entirely.

The duckweeds, hornwort or foxtail, nitella, water sprite, salvinia, riccia, azolla and the various dwarf lilies are examples of this group. All these plants require bright light. They can create a problem if allowed to grow too densely, for they will shade out the light from the lower area of the aquarium. For hiding areas to be used by young fishes, they are quite useful. They are also pastures for microorganisms that serve as a source of food for many fry.

Above: A well-planted community tank can accentuate the setting of any room. **Facing page:** In addition to their esthetic value, aquarium plants facilitate and are essential to the breeding of many aquarium fish species. Photo by M. Palicka.

Rooted Plants

The foremost group of plants is the so-called rooted class. Many of the common aquarium plants fall into this group, which can be further divided into the tape-grass, group-plant, and center-plant types.

The tape grasses are so called because they have long ribbonlike leaves. They also tend to have root systems that are relatively small in proportion to their overall size. Thus, they can be planted together closely without suffering unduly from competition. The two genera that we shall consider here are *Vallisneria* and *Sagittaria*. These two groups resemble each other closely, but they are not closely related, belonging to different families of plants. It should also be pointed out that they do not prosper as a rule if kept in the same aquarium. Kept together, both types will show slower growth and often die, with the *Vallisneria* usually going first.

Under the genus *Vallisneria*, we usually encounter three species for the aquarium, namely *V. spiralis*, *V. gigantea*, and *V. spiralis torta*.

Vallisneria spiralis is so called because the female plant sends up a flower to the surface on a long spiraling stem. The male plant, on the other hand, has a small club-shaped flower that remains near the crown, releasing pollen that floats to the surface to fertilize the female plant. In this genus a plant is either male or female. Both male and female plants also reproduce by sending out runners, and they can do this quite vigorously in the aquarium. This plant is the most versatile and the hardiest of the group.

Vallisneria spiralis torta, corkscrew vallisneria, is a variety of the foregoing plant. Its leaves have a definite spiral pattern, which is quite attractive. It usually does not exceed eight to ten inches in the aquarium. Set in groups it is quite attractive. Almost as versatile as *V. spiralis*, it tends to do better with bright light and alkaline water.

Vallisneria gigantea, jungle vallisneria, is less commonly encountered than the other two plants, and small specimens may be easily confused with *V. spiralis*. Such confusion does not last long, however, for this plant quickly lives up to its name and gets big. The leaves can grow to over one yard in length, winding this way and that, or else poking up out of the water and dying off. For a huge aquarium it is a splendid background plant, but it is otherwise unsuitable for the average hobbyist.

Species of the genus *Sagittaria* are not as easy to classify and describe as those of *Vallisneria*. For one thing, there are more varieties of them, and, for another, there seems to be little agreement in the various sources available as to their exact classification. It is noteworthy to recall that members of the closely related swordplant genus *Echinodorus* have sometimes been mistakenly classified as *Sagittaria* species. Even botanists commonly disagree among themselves on the names of some of these plants.

The *Sagittaria* plants do not have the separate sexes as do the *Vallisneria*. They reproduce mainly by runners, sometimes flowering and producing seeds. The flowers are produced at or above the water level and are more showy than *Vallisneria* flowers. Usually these plants produce leaves before they flower, but this is not invariable. Flowering is uncommon under typical aquarium conditions.

Sagittaria subulata is the most commonly encountered member of this genus in the aquarium. It varies considerably and is classified by some botanists into sub-species, which others identify as separate species. The plant resembles *Vallisneria spiralis* closely in size and shape, but it has slightly narrower and denser leaves. This is usually the plant that people are thinking of when they say *Sagittaria*. It will grow to over one foot in length in the aquarium, and it tends to "tailor its size" to the water level. This plant will flower in the aquarium more commonly than any of the other *Sagittaria* species. It is sometimes identified as *S. natans* or *S. subulata natans*.

Sagittaria subulata pusilla, sometimes called *S. pusilla*, is often referred to in the trade as the "needle sag." It has quite narrow, thin leaves and rarely exceeds eight inches in height. Thus it is a good plant for small aquaria.

Sagittaria filiformis, also known as *S. gracilis*, is a little smaller and narrower leafed than *S. subulata*. Otherwise it is quite similar and requires the same care.

Sagittaria platyphylla differs somewhat in appearance from the standard tape-grass form of this genus. It has broad, flat, fairly thick leaves, growing up to ten inches in length. This plant creates a fountainlike effect and can be used as an effective centerpiece in a small aquarium or as a striking group plant in a larger one. It tends to reproduce vigorously by sending off runners in all directions at the same time, rather than one or two at a time, as is the usual case in the other members of this genus.

Sagittaria eatonii resembles the foregoing plant. It is smaller and has narrower leaves, but the fountainlike effect is notable in that the leaves spread laterally, rather than grow straight up and down. This plant frequently grows into nice lawnlike groups in the aquarium. This one does not produce emersed leaves when it flowers, for the blooms are held above the water's surface and are described as having crimson undersides.

There are other *Sagittaria* species that are occasionally found in

Above: One of the many varieties of the popular *Sagitarria subulata.* **Facing page:** *Vallisneria spiralis torta*, also called *V. tortissima*, is a rather hardy plant that grows particularly well in bright light and moderately alkaline water. Photos by R. Zukal.

aquaria, or else are grown in outdoor ponds or as bulbs, planted in water, growing up into the air and blooming.

In general, all tape grasses require moderate to bright lighting, clean water not too loaded with nitrogenous wastes, and a temperature range between 70 and 80°F. In general, the *Sagittaria* species will do a little better at the lower end of this range, whereas the *Vallisneria* species seem to do as well at the warmer end.

The next genus for us to consider is the swordplants or *Echinodorus* species. These plants vary from the smallest of plants used in the aquarium to some of the largest. There are many species, but the descriptions offered here will be confined to those plants suitable for ordinary aquarium use.

Echinodorus intermedius, known as the dwarf swordplant, is one of the easiest of aquatic plants to grow. It does best in relatively small aquaria and likes bright lighting, growing in compact rosettes and reproducing very rapidly. In fact, this is the one drawback about the plant, since it can quickly overrun a tank if not thinned out regularly. In dimmer light or in deeper tanks, leaves become longer and growth is slowed.

Echinodorus tenellus, a variable plant, exists in two forms. The longer form, which hails from the more temperate areas of its range, is commonly sold as the "junior sword." This plant resembles a short *Vallisneria spiralis* more than anything else, likes moderate to bright lighting, and reproduces rapidly with runners growing above the sand. The runners are red in color. The shorter, or tropical form, is usually sold as "dwarf sagittaria" and has been misidentified as *Sagittaria microfolia* for years. This plant rarely exceeds 1.5 inches in length and looks very much like a grass lawn in the aquarium. It is thus a very useful plant for groups in the foreground of small- to medium-sized tanks.

Echinodorus brevipedicellatus, the Amazon sword, has long been considered the queen of aquatics. It is also called the "narrow-leafed" sword. The petioles, or leaf stems, are much shorter in this plant than in any of the larger varieties of the genus, and this fact gives the unique and striking effect of a great compact fountain of leaves rising up from the sand. Leaf and stem can be as long as 18 inches, so this beauty needs a tall 20-gallon aquarium at least to accommodate its full-grown size. In smaller aquaria the leaves will trail along the surface and dry out. Reproduction is by runners that trail out into the water and may rise above it. Young plants are produced along the breeding spike. Any plant in good condition will reproduce, no matter what you hear about "mother" or "female" plants. The truth is that the same plant produces reproductive structures of both sexes. Flowering by this plant is quite common in the aquarium. A moderate light is preferred. The author finds that it will adapt successfully to a variety of water conditions, although soft acidic water is ideal, preferably kept in the mid-70s or low 80s on the Fahrenheit scale, with relatively clean water, which should be regularly changed. This plant is quite susceptible to the effects of prolonged bottom filtering and should be potted if this method of filtration is used, which can be said for the other large members of this genus as well.

Echinodorus rangerii, called the broad-leafed sword, is quite similar to the foregoing plant, except that it is a larger plant, with the combined leaf and pedicel over two feet in length in the mature specimen. Pedicels are somewhat longer in proportion to the leaves. In all other respects the two plants are quite similar. This plant requires a large aquarium, a tall 25-gallon being the minimum for it. Certainly it is well displayed in a 50- or even 100-gallon tank.

Echinodorus martii has leaves that are long, narrowish and wavy, with a definite ruffled effect, hence the name "ruffled sword." The general shape of this plant is more tallish than spread out, as are the narrow- and broad-leafed swords. Besides the unique leaf shape, it possesses another quite desirable characteristic, namely the breeding spike, or inflorescence, which is sturdier than the similar structures that other aquatic plants develop; this breeding spike is carried up and out of the water. Even in the open air it reacts very little to dryness, and it produces a quite showy cluster of small plants, which can be removed, submerged, and cultivated. Even more striking are the white flowers that are borne at the same time as the platelets form.

Care and maintenance are the same as for *E. brevipedicellatus*, except that a larger tank is eventually needed, and some opening for the breeding spike should be provided when it develops. This plant may also reproduce by flowers, and it will sometimes bud at the crown, producing a young plant by the crown of the older one. This characteristic is also true of the narrow- and broad-leafed swordplants, but it is less often seen.

Echinodorus argentinensis, known to the trade as the "melon sword," is aptly named. The leaves are broad and oval, with prominent veining suggestive of the white stripes on one variety of watermelon. The stems are quite long in proportion to the large leaves, and the plant is thus somewhat "leggy."

Echinodorus rostratus and *E. cordifolius* are compatible species of this group that are quite similar in appearance and are commonly sold as "alismas" or "cellophane plants." They are called this because their leaves are quite translucent and crinkled, thus resembling cellophane. For a brief period they will put on quite a show in the aquarium, producing leaves of quite varied shapes on the same plant as they grow taller. Eventually, however, all their leaves will be floating and then emersed, leaving only the stems

Left: *Aponogeton fenestralis*, the Madagascar lace plant, together with other plant species. Photo by W. Tomey. **Below:** Collection of *Cryptocoryne* and other species.

Facing page: Spawning against a backdrop of Java Fern, *Microsorium pteropus*. Photos by H.J. Richter.

visible in the aquarium.

Echinodorus radicans, which was once misidentified as *Sagittaria quayanensis*, is quite a spectacular plant. It, like the cellophane plants, is a bog plant, growing with the big, variable leaves emersed. In warmer parts of the U.S., it is a popular pond plant. It can be kept in the aquarium for some time. The trick is to grow it in a small aquarium until the leaves begin to emerge from the water, and then transfer it to a larger one, keeping it in fairly dim light. This slows it down for a while, but eventually it grows out of the water and then shows only stems. It is so spectacular that for years people were willing to go to the trouble of keeping it just for its temporary beauty, wishing that it were possible to keep it submerged. It grows to about two feet in height, with large heart-shaped leaves which vary in size and number of nervures, or "veins" in the leaf.

Echinodorus tunicatus, in the author's opinion, is the most beautiful plant of the genus. It could be called the *radicans* that does not grow out of the water; but this would be falling short of an adequate description. The broad, heart-shaped leaves are borne up on

about four inches in length, and the leaves are up to eight inches long and five wide. All mature leaves have exactly seven nervures. In moderate to bright light the leaves tend to grow parallel with the bottom, and are a pleasing light green in color. New leaves are first a brick-red, changing through yellowish to pea-green as they unfurl. As if this were not enough, the miniature plants send up breeding spikes. Each spike has three nodes, each of which produces three white flowers that open and bloom under water. Each node will also produce one—rarely two—young plants. Water hardness is not important, and it will flourish in mildly acid to very alkaline water. Moderate to bright lighting is necessary.

The genus *Aponogeton* requires a little more care than does any of the foregoing. The ones we shall describe are large plants, all quite suitable for striking centerpieces in the aquarium. They have a large central bulblike structure, or rhizome, and all go through a period of dormancy in midwinter. They should be stored at low temperatures if it is expected that they will return with the vigor previously shown.

Reproduction is usually by seeding from the blooms, more rarely from division or budding of the rhizome. In general they do better in soft water that is frequently changed, but this is not essential in every case. We have seen some splendid specimens that have grown in hard water, usually in the low 70s° F.

Aponogeton crispus x *undulatus* hybrids are the most commonly available specimens of this genus. Somewhat variable, of course, they tend to produce long, narrow, regularly crimped or ruffled leaves, which are wavy and up to 18 inches in length, some varieties remaining smaller. This plant is a heavy feeder, and the sand should be well loaded with mulm, as in an established tank, or else some clay should be added to the sand at the time of planting. Color varies from light to bright green, and some reddish varieties have been produced, which are usually on the smaller side. Lighting should be moderate. Temperature should be in the 60s° F. during the relatively dormant period of mid-winter. Water hardness is not too important, for these plants have been widely cultivated and adapted in the process. Blooming of tiny white flowers on a vertical and fully emersed stalk is quite common, even in the aquarium.

Aponogeton ulvaceus, a broad-leafed, strikingly beautiful plant, is occasionally available. Full-grown leaves are over one foot long and three inches wide, translucent and slightly wavy. A large aquarium is needed for this one, and it dies down in mid-winter, at which time it should be kept cool, in the 60s° F. It produces a single spike of creamy to yellowish small flowers, very similar to the plant previously described.

Aponogeton fenestralis, the fabulous Madagascar lace plant, is the most striking but most difficult-to-grow member of the genus. A review of the literature on this one reveals all sorts of advice which is immediately contradicted in the next article that one encounters. A good specimen is truly striking, however, with leaves up to one foot in length, borne up on stems four inches or more long. The network of veins is completely open, with no leaf tissue in between, giving a screen-wire or "lace" effect. Young leaves, which are rapidly produced when the plant hits its stride, should be a light pinkish hue, turning darker as they unfurl. Our own experience has been best when this plant has been cultured in soft, slightly acidic water, kept in the low 70s° F and frequently changed. This plant's rhizome is highly susceptible to rot; therefore, the sand should be quite clean around it. In mid-winter the plant dies down and usually fails to return with any vigor; but it is said that it will if the bulb is stored in the low 60s° F. Sometimes a new plant will develop next to the old, and we have had one successful experience at separating a young plant from the old and having it grow. This one puts out an inflorescence with a double, horseshoe-shaped flower stalk, covered with tiny white flowers. A very similar lace plant, *A. henkelianus*, is sometimes encountered. It has a denser network of veins and is more pinkish green. Flower and general requirements are similar to *A. fenestralis*.

Last in this group of plants is the *Cryptocoryne*, which are not really true aquatics, spending part of their lives with leaves emersed during dry seasons, and submerged in rainy seasons. They can tolerate long periods of submerged existence and can be successfully cultivated as aquatic plants if some care is taken

Above: This attractive layout follows several aquascaping principles, including large background plants with smaller foreground plants and contrasting leaf shapes and colorations. **Facing page:** Most specialists agree that healthy plants contribute both physiologically and psychologically to fishes' well-being. Photos by B. Kahl.

to provide them with proper conditions. Most of the varieties described here reproduce by short runners or budding along the "corm" or central bulblike structure. Three varieties will bloom underwater. They are quite variable as to appearance, coloration and requirements; but, in general, they like warm temperatures 75° F and up, soft water, moderate lighting, fertile (not foul) sand, and quiet water. The older varieties to be cultivated are less exacting than the newer ones, as far as water conditions are concerned.

Cryptocoryne nevillii, the smallest member of this genus that we shall consider, has been misidentified for years as *C. beckettii*. This plant is small, varying in height from a little over one inch (small form) to about four inches (tall form). The spear-shaped leaves are vivid green on the surface, paler beneath. This plant tends to form dense carpets on the bottom in time and likes moderate light. Over-lighting will shortly be followed by paling to a yellowish color and "crawling"; that is, flattening out on the sand.

Cryptocoryne beckettii, usually sold in the U.S. as "cordata," is a somewhat larger plant, growing up to six inches high. The leaves are fairly narrow- or lance-shaped with pinkish to reddish undersides. Moderate lighting is good.

Cryptocoryne willisii could be called the "technicolor crypt." The narrow, wavy leaves are usually light green with reddish markings; but they may be yellowish or reddish above as well as below. We have seen adult specimens that were almost jet black above and reddish purple below. Full-size specimens are about eight inches long. Lighting is moderate to bright, with tolerance to lighting greater than in the foregoing species described. This species, however, is quite sensitive to excessive aeration. As it grows, the central stem gets longer, and the new plants usually emerge along it, rather than being formed on runners.

Cryptocoryne griffithii is a fairly large plant, growing up to over one foot in height. The broad, heart-shaped leaves are carried on long, erect stems, turning outward parallel with the bottom. This plant, like all the other broad-leafed crypts, is quite sensitive to over-lighting. If the leaves begin to bend down towards the sand, then decrease light intensity at once. Otherwise the plant "crawls," turns yellow, develops transparent places in the leaves, rots, and disintegrates within a matter of days. Twenty watts of overhead lighting in a standard ten-gallon tank is sufficient. Strong side lighting has a tendency to distort the growth of this and similar crypts, thus it should be avoided. Color of the leaves is a dark, shiny green above, lighter below. Reddish stippling is sometimes seen, more on the undersurfaces. This plant produces a submerged flower, the long spathe of which is blackish purple. Reproduction in the aquarium is by short rooted runners. Rarely are more than several young plants produced in a year. Soft acid water is best.

Cryptocoryne cordata is a similar broad-leafed plant. Often hard to distinguish from *C. griffithii*, it is a slightly taller plant and does tend to have more color in the leaves, the undersides of which may be reddish purple in color. The upper leaf surfaces are variable in color from dark green to bluish gray, showing more stippling with black in the gray-colored leaves. This plant blooms and reproduces very much as does *C. griffithii* but the bloom may have yellow on all or part of the spathe. Conditions for maintenance are much the same as for the foregoing. This plant makes a splendid centerpiece for aquaria up to 20 gallons in size.

Cryptocoryne ciliata comes in two varieties: major, a plant growing up to 18 inches tall; and minor, usually remaining under 8 inches. It has lanceolate, apple-green leaves which are lighter on the underside. Moderate to bright lighting is enjoyed. This is one of the easiest of the crypts to maintain, but it reproduces quite slowly in the aquarium.

Cryptocoryne haerteliana is a plant that tends to spread horizontally as a rule. Its leaves, which grow to several inches on a short, sturdy stem, are silky green above, with prominent nervures, and rosy pink below. It reproduces rapidly, forming dense groves or groups that create a pleasing effect.

Cryptocoryne longicauda is truly the most unusual member of this group. Large heart-shaped leaves up to four inches long and almost as wide are carried on short, thick stems. The upperside of the leaves is ashy green; the underside is almost gray. The large leathery leaves have a crinkled texture, much as is caused in a balled-up piece of paper. This plant is very particular in its requirements, and extremely sensitive to light, "crawling" and rotting under conditions of moderate lighting. Thus, light should be dim.

Cryptocoryne somphongsis is the tallest member of the genus to be considered in this book. It has long, narrow, closely rippled leaves which vary from light to dark green. The central rib of the leaf is often red, giving the appearance of rhubarb, thus the name "rhubarb crypt." This plant does well in all kinds of water, including hard alkaline. It survives and grows in the 50s° F.

Cryptocoryne blassii is one of the newer crypts to be imported. It very much resembles *C. griffithii* in general structure but it gets a bit taller and tends to have leaves somewhat smaller and narrower than *C. griffithii*. Color is most striking in this plant, for the upper leaf is purplish red to bronzish, while the lower side is pink. This plant needs moderate lighting and does best in soft acid water.

Above: A handsome *Cryptocoryne cordata* specimen displaying its appealing leaf coloration. **Facing page:** The spathe of a *C. beckettii* specimen; the spathe is a modified leaf structure that plays a vital role in the plant's reproduction. Photos by L. Wischnath.

Bunch Plants

The bunch plants have already been described in structure. They are quite useful in the aquarium because they can be trained into tall stands of plants that make excellent backgrounds or end plantings. As a group, they do better with bright lighting and prosper if some natural sunlight is provided. They can be pruned or trained around solid objects in the aquarium to create beautiful effects. Quite variable in shape, color and requirements, most are quite easy to maintain and reproduce. Most of them strive toward the surface of the aquarium, from which they will put out emersed or aerial leaves and bloom. All can be easily reproduced from cuttings.

One of the oldest bunch plants used in the aquarium is the genus *Elodea*, frequently misidentified as "anacharis," which also serves as a common name in the hobby for this group of plants. Another common name for this plant is "goldfish weed," for it is often sold with goldfish and will keep well at the cooler temperatures that goldfish prefer, namely around the 60s° F. Kept warmer, this plant becomes pale, stringy and falls apart. The foregoing refers to *E. canadensis.* A South American species, *E. densa* is described and said to be more tolerant of "tropical" aquarium conditions. This plant produces new plants as runners and stems, branching out from the nodes, and occasionally will send up small flowers in the aquarium. It can be rooted or allowed to float free on the surface.

Limnophila, frequently misidentified as *Ambulia*, is one of the most beautiful of the bunch plants, growing in light-green rosettes of finely divided leaves on tall stems. It reproduces freely by sending out runners, both from the base and along the length of the stem. This plant is well displayed in tall aquaria and creates beautiful effects if daylight strikes the front of the aquarium. The only drawback to it is that it usually does poorly in hard water. Three species of this genus have been described, *L. heterophylla, L. sessiflora*, and *L. gratioloides*; the last one is said to be toxic to fishes if the stems are divided in the water. We have suffered no losses or discernible injuries to fishes which were kept with this plant when it was cut back. However, many reliable observers have, so caution should be used with *L. gratioloides.*

Cabomba, also known as Washington grass, resembles the foregoing plants in general form, but has a darker green color and forms larger rosettes of the finely divided leaves. In general, we have found it to be more tolerant of hard water than *Limnophila*. It does not branch as freely, however. The best species for aquarium cultivation is *C. aquatica*, which is more tolerant of the warmth. A reddish variety, *C. caroliniana pulcherrima*, is occasionally offered for sale and is suitable for cooler aquaria. The red color is maintained only under very bright lighting.

Ludwigia is represented by a number of species offered to the aquarist, most of which are moderately suitable for the aquarium. This is because of their high-light but low-temperature requirements, plus the fact that they tend to be bog plants in nature and tolerate prolonged submersing poorly. Fortunately there are some exceptions to the rule, and these make a beautiful addition to the scene if planted and maintained in large groves or banks in the aquarium. *L. natans* is probably the best, especially if the plants originate from the southern part of its range. The narrow, slightly wavy leaves are glossy green above, bright pink below. Bright light and a bottom well saturated with droppings are good; no special water conditions are required.

Hygrophila polysperma, an old standby, has long been considered one of the best bunch plants there is. The leaves are a pleasing light green color above, lighter below. Moderate to bright lighting and any water conditions suffice. This plant is somewhat sensitive to excessive concentrations of nitrogenous substances in the water and will show this by producing darker green coiled and deformed new leaves. This plant becomes bushy with pruning and the cuttings establish rapidly.

Synnema triflorum is the most recently imported bunch plant to come into common use in the U.S. Usually sold as "water wisteria," this superb plant shows the most striking variation of leaf form, going from slightly serrated small ovals to multi-lobed irregular large leaves that give a stag-horn effect. As a rule, the taller the plant, the more lobes on the leaves, with the most recently produced leaves having the most lobes.

Myriophyllum is a genus represented by several species available at times, none of which is a particularly good aquarium plant, except for *M. pinnatum*. This is a bushy plant that withstands the usual temperatures encountered in the aquarium and has no particular water requirements. It is somewhat difficult to distinguish this plant from others of the genus on sight, but the others will disintegrate in a short time, while *M. pinnatum* will prevail. For coldwater aquaria, *M. elatinoides, M. hippuroides*, and *M. spicatum* are satisfactory, but they will not last very long when kept at temperatures in the 70s° F.

Above: *Elodea canadensis*, commonly called anacharis, is a temperate-water plant that does best when kept in water ranging in the 60s° F. Photo by L. Wischnath. **Facing page:** *Myriophyllum spicatum*, also a temperate-water plant that typically will not do well in water kept above 70° F. Photo by R. Zukal.

Floating Plants

The floating plants can be divided into two main categories: those that are rooted in the sand but have emersed leaves; and those that float free, roots and all. In the former group we shall consider the various dwarf tropical lilies that are frequently offered for sale. Some temperate-zone plants are included in this grouping as well, but they typically do poorly in tropical aquaria, adapting better to colder tanks, such as those for goldfish. The tropicals are usually in the genus *Nymphaea* and the temperates are in the genus *Nuphar*. They are sold respectively as tropical or "Madagascar lilies" and as "spatterdocks." Both forms begin as submerged plants, often with colorful leaves that for a time are very attractive. Sooner or later, though, floating and emersed leaves are produced, leaving only stems visible through the sides of the tank. Even a fairly large aquarium will soon have its entire surface covered by the leaves, while the sandy bottom is thoroughly infiltrated by masses of roots, which can create problems for other plants—if there are any left—for they are deprived of light and must struggle for root absorption of nutriment. It is a good idea to pot these fellows, for they will do as well and yet not crowd out the other plants. The spatterdocks are noted by the presence of a bulb or "corm," which should be firm all over. The tendency to rot is quite marked in this group, but cooler temperatures and acid water tend to reduce the chances of this happening. The lilies often bloom in the aquarium, producing perfect little water-lily blooms in emersed stalks. We have observed both white and violet blooms which lasted one day and were very fragrant.

The genus *Lemna*, commonly known as "duckweed," is represented by the three species *L. minor, L. gibbosa,* and *L. trisulca*. *L. minor* and *L. gibbosa* float at the water surface, and *L. trisulca* floats just below it. All three species will reproduce vigorously if given plenty of light and kept from of animals that will eat them. They can cover the surface, causing no problems of oxygen exchange but cutting out the light necessary to the plants below. Periodic thinning out is necessary and can become a nuisance. These plants are undoubtedly useful for feeding plant-eating fishes.

The genus *Ceratophyllum* is represented by the two species *C. submersum* and *C. demersum*, commonly known as foxtail and hornwort. These plants are remarkable for their lack of roots, tending to float just below the surface, growing at one end and dying off at the other. New branches are formed from the nodes at various points along the length of the central stem. It is a rapidly growing plant of rather pleasing form, looking for all the world like a branch of evergreen. Color of *C. submersum* is a light green, and the leaves are longer and more spread out than *C. demersum*, which is darker, with the leaves more densely clustered. Bright light is required. In general, this plant prefers hard water, and it can be said to grow under conditions that are unsuitable for most other aquarium plants.

An old favorite is *Ceratopteris thalictroides*, commonly called water sprite, an aquatic fern that requires only bright light and warm temperatures. Young plants are formed on the edges of the viviparous leaves and do best if allowed to float until fully formed. This plant may be rooted in sand, where it forms a tall, spectacular plant, up to 18 inches high. Rooting is best accomplished when the fern is first allowed to develop as a floater until the leaves are several inches long. Roots are very sensitive to putrefaction in the sand and will rot away if the bottom is not very clean. Because of this property, it is used by fish breeders, especially keepers of fancy guppies, to act as a check on sand conditions. If allowed to float, water sprite will send up aerial leaves that are very narrow and branched, looking very much like a deer's antlers. Two varieties exist, narrow- and broad-leafed; the broad-leafed form is encountered more often and is somewhat more vigorous in growth. It is one of the finest and most useful of aquatic plants. Its only drawback is that it survives only a year; but this is more than overcome by its reproducing many times, thus leaving dozens of youngsters to continue and reproduce themselves.

Another fern occasionally encountered in the aquarium is the genus *Azolla*, which is represented by the two species, *A. caroliniana,* and *A. filiculoides,* temperate and tropical species respectively. Both are really more suited to outdoor culture but will survive in aquaria for a time.

Salvinia is another floating aquatic fern, but this one is much better suited for use in the aquarium, since it withstands the usual temperatures better.

Another old-timer is *Riccia fluitans*, an aquatic moss in which the small individual plants cluster together to form dense floating carpets on the water surface.

Nitella flexilis is another interesting floater. First of all, it is a complex, branching alga, thus not a true plant in the sense that it has roots, stems and leaves. Secondly, it will grow at all levels in the aquarium, thus forming lawns, banks, or clouds of delicate greenery. Thirdly, it can grow with less light than most of the floating group, but it should have at least moderate illumination.

Above: *Nuphar luteum*, commonly called a spatterdock, is a temperate dwarf lily. Photo by R. Zukal. **Facing page:** Floating plants, as well as plants that produce high-arcing leaves, can greatly facilitate the breeding of bubblenest-building fishes, such as *Pseudosphromenus dayi*. Photo by H.J. Richter.

Aquascaping

Under the individual description of the plant species covered, we mentioned some of their growth characteristics and occasionally made some suggestions as to their use in the aquarium. However, this work would be incomplete if the subject of aquarium design was not covered a bit more fully. After all, if a function of plants is to make a more attractive-looking setup, then it follows that some principles as to arrangement should be followed, as is true in terrestrial landscaping projects.

The first general point is that the taller plants should be set in back of the shorter ones, or else they should be placed at the sides of the aquarium to give a "frame" effect. Doing this creates a more naturalistic setting as well, and the background planting will set off or accentuate the plantings in front.

Secondly, the medium-sized plants, such as the smaller *Sagittaria* or the medium-sized *Cryptocoryne*, are excellent for the mid-ground of the aquarium. These look better when planted in groves or groups than when used individually. Many of the bunch plants, if trimmed to about half the height of the aquarium, also serve well in this way; this is especially true of *Hygrophila* and *Ludwigia*.

Next, the very small plants are usually lost in aquaria much over a foot deep. However, groves or lawns of these can be used effectively to set off the larger plants behind them or to soften the stark effects of rocks, wood pieces or ceramics. The smaller *Echinodorus tenellus*, *E. intermedius*, *Cryptocoryne nevillii*, and *Nitella flexilis* all find use in this manner. Another point is that the so-called centerplant, or largest plant specimen, is usually displayed most effectively if only one specimen is used. This is a fact, even in the larger aquaria. Also, it should not be exactly centered but set off to the left or right. If the center plant has long stems, a stone, piece of wood or ceramic device in front of it helps to soften this effect. Medium or smaller plants can then be used to break up the lines of the stone, wood or ceramic. Thus, a whole segment of design is created.

In addition to restating the fact that groups of plants look better than single ones—except for centerplants, of course—it is worthwhile to observe that the use of many different plants in the same aquarium is not wise. If more than three or four species are used, a "busy" or hodgepodge effect is likely, and further, the odds are that some of the plants will do poorly since it becomes more difficult to provide an equally healthy environment.

Beautiful aquaria can be achieved if no centerplant is used at all, but every aquarium should have a central point of interest, which can be accomplished with a striking rock, bit of drift wood or ceramic figure.

If an aquarium is set where there will be a significant amount of daylight striking it, the front glass should be toward the source of the daylight. This is because the plants—and especially the bunch plants—will turn towards the daylight and thus display best.

Any large or striking object will be distracting if its effect is not "softened" or somewhat interrupted by other plants or objects around or in front of it.

Unless the plants in front of the aquarium are only a few inches high, a space of at least two inches should be left between the front glass and the first plantings to provide better swimming room and a more effective view of the fishes and other contents.

Color contrasts in shades of green are good. Shape contrasts can be striking. An aquarium with a stand of *Limnophila* on one side and a grove of *Cryptocoryne griffithii* on the other, separated by a big piece of driftwood, is only one of an infinite number of ideas. All of which brings us to the last and most important point: first, know what your plants require; and second, use your imagination. Knowledge and imagination, plus the few basic principles outlined here, are all you need!

Bibliography

AQUARIUM PLANTS
By Dr. K. Rataj and T. Horeman
ISBN 0-87666-455-9
TFH H-966
Audience: Designed for use by aquarium hobbyists, horticulturists, botanist and students, this massive and very highly colorful book is the most complete volume ever published about aquarium plants. High school level.
Hardcover, 5½ x 8", 448 pages
244 color photos, 124 black and white photos

DR. AXELROD'S MINI-ATLAS OF FRESHWATER AQUARIUM FISHES
By Dr. Herbert R. Axelrod, Dr. Warren E. Burgess, Dr. Cliff W. Emmens, et. al
ISBN 0-86622-385-1
TFH H-1090
The entire staff of TROPICAL FISH HOBBYIST magazine, aided by Prof. C. W. Emmens, pooled their talents to make this the most complete book on aquarium fishes ever published!
Hardcover, 5½ x 8½", 992 pages
Over 2200 full-color photos

YOUR HOME AQUARIUM
By Jorg Vierke
ISBN 0-86622-075-5
TFH TS-139
Audience: This is an excellent guide for anyone interested in starting a home aquarium. Touches on all important topics of maintenance and fish care, including water chemistry and setting up a balanced tank.
Hardcover, 8½ x 11", 144 pages
Over 240 full-color photos and drawings